THE ONE-HOUR CONTENT PLAN

THE ONE-HOUR CONTENT PLAN

THE SOLOPRENEUR'S GUIDE TO A YEAR'S WORTH OF BLOG POST IDEAS IN 60 MINUTES AND CREATING CONTENT THAT SELLS AND HOOKS.

MEERA KOTHAND

MEERA KOTHAND

"Where Marketing Meets Simple So Solopreneurs & Small Business Owners Can Build an Unmissable Standout Online Presence Minus the Sleaze"

WWW.MEERAKOTHAND.COM

Copyright © 2017 Meera Kothand

CONTENTS PAGE

You can download the content plan as well as the
bonus resources at 1HCP.ME/BONUS

THE BIG, BOLD PROMISE

I promised you a year of blog post ideas in a single hour.

Big, bold promise. I know.

And you may be tempted to download the One-Hour Content Plan templates and start filling them out.

But before you jet off in that direction, hear me out.

You can't jab at the One-Hour Content Plan with your blinders on.

So if you jump ahead, you're going to find a template that you aren't sure how to tackle. Before you begin, you need to know exactly how you're going to formulate your plan. That's how this book is going to help you.

Remember this quote?

Give a man a fish and you feed him for a day; teach a man to fish and you feed him for a lifetime.

Rather than feed you with fill-in-the blank templates (as juicy as they are), you're going to discover a method of generating content ideas *yourself.* And *then* I'll walk you through how you can fill in the One-Hour Content Plan.

Because let's be honest for a second, shall we?

All those guides that you hoard...the ones that promise you 100-200+ blog post ideas...

The Pinterest infographics with fill in the blank templates that you save...

The blog posts you read on *how to* come up with blog posts ideas...

While it's weirdly satisfying getting your hands on one of these (believe me I know, I've done them all)

And sure, they do tide you through for a little bit...

But *that* day will come where you'll still find yourself staring at the blank screen – the blogger's arch nemesis.

And it's oh–so familiar because you've been in this situation before.

All those headline formulas and templates you've stuffed your hard drive with – which promised to last you two years by the way – don't come to the rescue at all.

You know why?

Because the problem isn't that you have no content ideas....or you don't know *what* to create.

The problem is that you don't have a *strategy* or *system for* coming up with content ideas.

Two different things, right?

The lack of content ideas is just a symptom of a larger problem at hand. You can't just treat the symptom. You need to treat the underlying problem.

This is where the majority of people are stuck and where a blog content plan comes to the rescue.

3 Tell-Tale Signs You're in Desperate Need of a Blog Content Plan

1. You never know what to write.
On most days you struggle to come up with ideas and haven't planned in advance what your content is going to be about.

You're always looking to *fill* a publishing queue. You're producing content in a vacuum with no real thought as to how that content contributes to your blog or business goals.

2. You chase after content trends.
Your content topics sway from A-Z. You go after what you think will make your post go viral or get more shares.

There isn't necessarily a thread in any of your content pieces and they are random at best. You're hoping one or the other will take off and get a flood of traffic.

3. Your content doesn't have a strong link to the products or services you offer.
You're not sure how to create content to promote your products or services.

Whether you already have offers or you're thinking of creating one, your content doesn't connect you and the problem your reader is trying to solve.

Quick disclaimer: All content doesn't have to be filled with heavy calls to action that scream *buy*. Your content can also inspire and entertain your readers.

Whatever your goals are, your content has to contribute to inching the reader forward in the direction of your end goal. And this is something that you may be sorely missing.

The One-Hour Content Plan is about treating the underlying problem and arming you with a powerful **content strategy** for your blog.

It's going to help you unlock dozens of content possibilities with ease…to be exact, a full year's worth of traffic-building content ideas in 60 minutes or less…

Show your reader a clear path to your products and services…

Discover what topics your audience wants so you'll have direction and focus…

Help establish your brand…

And ultimately support the growth of your blog and business.

What exactly is a content strategy?
Demian Farnworth, chief content writer at Copyblogger, defined it this way: A content strategy is "a plan for building an audience by publishing, maintaining, and spreading frequent and consistent content that educates, entertains, or inspires to turn strangers into fans and fans into customers."

Without getting muddled in terms and definitions, content marketing is building a relationship with your reader by empowering and educating them via content. And content strategy is the plan that gets you there.

Easy enough, don't you think?

Content strategy isn't just for B2B and B2C companies. A content strategy is also a powerful tool for bloggers and solopreneurs.

What are the benefits of a content strategy?

Since our brains are wired to seek out the tangible benefits, let's start with those first.

Tangible Benefits of a Solid Content Strategy

SEO

The more exceptional content you publish, the more you get linked to from other people's blogs. The backlink sends a message to Google that your site has quality content.

Traffic

When you create exceptional content, people will come to your site and tell their friends about it too. When you get more traffic, it'll be easier for you to negotiate terms for sponsored posts and work with brands.

Sponsorship Opportunities

If your content has a direct link to a certain type of product or service, or if you write for a niche audience, you look immensely favorable in the eyes of brands who are constantly looking for influencers and bloggers to promote their suite of products and services.

Sales

The more purposeful content you put out there, the more your audience is able to connect you with the solution they are looking for. They're going to be ready to take their wallets out for you because you've primed them for the sale. This works the same way for affiliate products and services.

List Growth
If you create focused content (and lead magnets) that your audience wants, you'll have more people opting into your list.

Intangible Benefits of a Content Strategy

Awareness
Imagine this conversation in a Facebook group between your subscriber and a stranger.

Stranger: I'm so confused with Pinterest. Nothing I do ever works.

Your Subscriber: Have you checked out her blog? She's great at Pinterest and has a free course too. Here's a link.

Stranger: I so need to get my Pinterest in order! Let me check out the free course.

When you create content that empowers your audience, they'll pass links and recommendations to others without you even asking.

Respect and Adoration
It obviously takes time to build gushing fans because you need to earn their trust first. But once you've proven that you can help solve their problems, you're going to be their

'go to' source of information over the competition. Interviews for podcasts, guest posts, summits - you're going to be sought out for all of these as well. And the recommendations are going to come pouring in from your very own readers.

Mindshare Leading to Indirect Sales

They might not be in the market to buy your product or service right now, but when they do need a coach, a VA, a designer or a social media course, guess who's going to come to their mind first? It's you, of course, and that's because your content has grabbed mindshare.

Positioning Yourself as a Thought Leader or Expert

If you consistently over deliver with the content you create and go deep into a select few content categories, you'll be able to position yourself as the 'go-to' person for this topic.

How the One-Hour Content Plan Works

In the first section of this book, you're going to set the bearings for your **Content GPS**. You will lay a foundation for content success by defining the parameters within which your blog will exist.

You'll start to view your blog as a powerful driver of change for your audience and how you can use it to inject a distinctive point of view in your content.

In the second section of the book, you'll grasp three core ways to come up with content ideas — what I call the

E.O.G (Expert-Offer-Goal) **Method** Through this method you'll create timely content that empowers your reader and helps you sell your products and services.

Then the magic happens. You'll start putting this together in the One-Hour Content Plan.

In the third section of the book, you'll dissect your blog post into eight critical pieces and optimize each of them so your readers are hooked till the end of your page. The cherry on top – you'll get crystal clear on what your brand voice is using the **ADDE** (Attribute Markers - Do's - Dont's - Expressions) **Formula**.

In the last two sections, you'll discover strategies to promote your content and tools to help you make the editorial process easier.

No wishy washy definitions.

No guesses.

No hair pulling necessary.

But ignoring a content plan for your blog is the biggest mistake you can make.

Imagine for a minute how your blog and business would change if you never run out of blog post ideas...

You know exactly what to create, when to create it, and what results it'll drive.

Every single piece of content has a purpose in growing your blog and business, selling your products and services for you, and building your online presence…

Your offers (paid and free) become seductive magnets of YES! that readers cannot resist.

That's the power of a content strategy and the premise behind the One-Hour Content Plan.

Intrigued yet?

Welcome to a way of thinking and acting that most bloggers and solopreneurs are not accustomed to!

You'll never view content in the same way again. And this is exactly what's going to help you cut through the noise.

Let's ditch the fill-in-the blank templates and create content that's unique to you and your blog.

If you're ready, let's go!

Section I

YOUR CONTENT GPS: HOW TO SET YOURSELF UP FOR CONTENT SUCCESS

"What road do I take?" asked Alice.

The cat asked, "Where do you want to go?"

"I don't know," Alice answered.

"Then," said the cat, "it really doesn't matter, does it?"

— Lewis Carroll, Alice's Adventures in Wonderland

Here's what this quote from Alice in Wonderland can teach you about creating content for your blog.

When you're not able able to articulate the direction you want your content to take your readers, it's difficult for your readers to understand where you're taking them too.

You can't throw darts at content repeatedly hoping something will stick. Throwing spaghetti at the wall is never the answer.

You have to get clear about why your blog exists.

In this section you'll learn how to set yourself up for content success by defining your blog parameters. You'll be introduced to the **Driver of Change (DoC)** concept, which is a powerful way of viewing your blog and business.

You'll walk away with a clear idea of the purpose of your content, as well as who you're writing for. You'll be the driver of your content rather than feel pressured to follow trends, get shares, or amass traffic. Your content will move you closer to the goals and vision *you* have set.

If you just started blogging, you may not have all the answers to the questions raised in this section. That's ok.

Your answers to these questions will develop over time as you better understand your niche, the products and

you want to create, as well as your target
.

You can download the content plan as well as the
bonus resources at 1HCP.ME/BONUS

Chapter 1

DEFINE YOUR CONTENT PLAYING FIELD

To get to the crux of your content playing field, let's start at the beginning by defining the niche that your blog and business serves.

In its essence, a niche is a solution to a problem. People want to be better versions of themselves. This better version does not have to be about having more money. It could be in any one of the following areas:

- Personal development
- Fitness
- Food
- Budgeting or Personal finance
- Fashion/Beauty
- Lifestyle
    - Home decor
    - Organization
    - Travel
    - Outdoor/Survival

Why do you blog or do business in any one of these niches? If you and I were to be honest, we would say to make money.

But beyond money, why does your blog exists. You can't blog in a vacuum.

Well you could, but then you wouldn't be reading this book now would you? You would be what we call a hobbyist. You write for yourself or close family. Not necessarily an audience.

But to make any money at all, you need to attract an audience to your blog. For most of us, our blogs exists for an audience. It's easier to define your niche in terms of who you serve and on what topic. This is where your value proposition or blog purpose comes in. This will form the basis of every single piece of content you create.

How can you come up with an all-encompassing purpose or value proposition for your blog?

First, answer these two questions:

1. What group do you want to help?
2. In what area do you want to help them? Or in what area do they struggle that you believe you can help them?

For example, let's say the group I want to help is women and the area or topic is healthy meal planning. I now have two big groups to work with. Break these groups down further. Try to get specific with your answers.

You're not helping just any women, but homeschooling moms. And you're not helping them plan meals, but paleo meals on a budget. Once you break it down in this way, your content angle takes on a very specific dimension.

Plug your specific answer into one of these statements.

I educate/inspire/entertain/teach/**help** _women_ who want to _know that they are enough Doing_
I show _wives &_ _moms_ how _____
embrace who they are _Sued_ _jobs_
& where they are at. _Freedom_

Once you've plugged in these pieces, you know why your blog really exists and who you're helping. This is your blog's purpose or value proposition.

Your Blog as a Driver of Change

Now that you have an overview of who you plan to serve with your blog, let's dive deeper and ask yourself what *change* your blog creates for your readers.

The **Driver of Change (DoC)** Model is a powerful way of thinking about your blog. Because when you think about everything you publish not simply as "content," but as a catalyst for specific change, your approach to blogging will shift. Content should transform your readers.

And that transformation should progress both you and your audience toward your respective goals.

The DoC model focuses on the **'Before,'** which is your reader's current state, and the **'After,'** which is where they'll be by implementing and consuming your content. You compare the readers' 'Before' and 'After' against three components:

1. What are your readers going through?
2. What do your readers feel?
3. What thoughts run through their minds?

For instance, I want to help my readers who are mostly solopreneurs and bloggers use email and craft a solid blogging strategy to earn an income, build authority and make an impact online. I want them to embrace email, have clearly defined goals and focus with their blogs and make progress every single quarter.

This is my change for my reader – the destination that my content and products will bring my reader towards. Here's how my example looks broken down into the three components.

What are your readers going through?
Before: Struggling to have blogging goals. Jump from one social media to another or one Facebook group to another. Don't know where to focus their time and efforts.

After: Clearly defined purpose. Know exactly what to focus on. Don't feel the pressure to be everywhere.

What do your readers feel?

Before: Confused. Lost. Overwhelmed.

After: In control. Like they are making progress every single day.

What thoughts run through their minds?

Before: My blog is never going to take off. Not knowing tech or design is keeping me from achieving my dreams. I don't even know what my blogging goals are. I know email is important, but I don't know how to get started with it.

After: I can do this. I will meet my goals if I take it one step at a time. I don't have to be on all social media platforms.

Do this exercise for your blog right now. Download a set of worksheets to help you here: 1HCP.ME/BONUS

Now that you're clear about how you're helping your readers, let's dive deeper.

You know the end-point. You know where you want your reader to be. What content can you produce that will help your reader get to this end point?

This is where you consider your content buckets.

Think of your content in terms of buckets.

Each content category is a bucket and you can have up to seven content buckets. Your content categories (buckets) will support your blog's overall message. And within each category you have sub-categories and topics.

For example, if you have a budget/frugal blog and the purpose is to help 30 to 40- somethings get out of debt, think about the content categories that will help the reader achieve that purpose. These could be budgeting, intentional living, saving/investing.

Or if you run a motherhood or parenting blog and the purpose of your blog is to help home-schooling parents be stress-free and raise confident learners, your categories could be organization, lesson plans and parenting.

If you are struggling to nail down your content buckets, head back to the core purpose or value proposition of your blog that you identified. What categories would support that purpose?

We'll break down our sub-category and topics in the next section. But for now, determine the purpose of your blog and your main content buckets.

Action Item:

Determine what your core blog categories are. Do the DoC Model exercise for your blog. There are a set of worksheets you can download at: 1HCP.ME/BONUS

Chapter 2

FIND AN IMAGINARY FRIEND IN YOUR IDEAL READER

Here's what Henneke Duistermaat in an article for Copyblogger has to say about the relationship you should have with your ideal reader.

"Your ideal reader should become like an imaginary friend. You should know your ideal reader so well that you can start a conversation with her at any time. You know when she shakes her head because you say something she doesn't agree with. You know what makes her smile or laugh. You know the questions she asks. You know how to charm and flatter her."

Content that tries to attract everyone attracts no one.

For your content to have a stronghold on your audience, you need to convince them that you know exactly what they're going through.

By defining who exactly your ideal reader is, you'll be able to:

- talk to your audience at the right level.
- not waste your effort writing for people who will never enjoy or gel with your content.
- not scratch your head thinking about what content to create because you know what your audience needs.

This is why you need a reader persona - an accurate description of your ideal reader. Beyond demographics, you need to dig into their psychographics and motivational factors.

Drew Eric Whitman, in his book Ca$hvertising, identifies eight basic desires that all human beings are born with and nine more that we learn. The following eight basic desires are intrinsic and biologically programmed:

- survival/enjoyment of life/life extension
- enjoyment of food and beverage
- freedom from pain, fear, and danger
- sexual companionship
- comfortable living conditions
- superiority/winning/keep up with the Joneses
- care and protection of loved ones
- social approval

In addition to these, we want to learn:

- to be informed
- to be curious

- to have clean bodies and surroundings
- efficiency
- convenience
- dependability/quality
- to express beauty and style
- economy/profit
- bargains

Think about how these manifest in your target audience. If they don't fulfill or achieve these desires, how would they feel and how will this be a source of fear or frustration for them. Taken together, all these questions will help you understand at a deeper level the type of person you want to attract and influence.

Here are a few hacks that I regularly use to spy on my audience without paying for expensive research.

Search Facebook Groups to Find Reader Motivations

Join Facebook groups where your ideal audience members are likely to hang out.

Once you have access to a Facebook group, use the "Search this group" box and type in the following keywords (preserving the quotes) followed by your topic:

- "need help"
- "desperate for"
- "newbie"

- "have no clue"
- "advice about"
- "question about"

This allows you to quickly zone in on your target audience's pain points without spending hours scouring through the feeds.

Look Outwards

If your current audience is small, don't hesitate to look beyond your own blog to gather data. Look at comments in other blogs in your niche. Use a tool like Buzzsumo to find content that is popular or viral in your space. Notice how people react to it. What are they saying? Pay close attention to the emotions it triggers and what needs it fulfills.

In my case, my audience are solopreneurs - bloggers, freelancers, one-person shop boutique owners, etc.

Many of them have fears and frustrations that they "will never grow an audience," "work hard but still not make a single cent," "never be able to create passive income," "be called out as a fraud," "not be seen as an expert," etc.

Under desires they want to "inspire and grow a community," "be appreciated," "be recognized by their peers," "make a full-time income from home," etc.

Once you list these fears and frustrations, you'll be able to use those clues to craft headlines and blog post openers that hook readers and tap into their deepest thoughts.

The following are actual examples of headlines and post openings I've used and that reflect my readers' frustrations.

Headline: What to send your email list: The beginner's guide for the clueless blogger

Blog post Opener:
"You're sitting in front of your screen.
Fingers on your keyboard.
The clock's ticking and this email has to go out in a couple of hours to your list.
As hard as you stare, your fingers aren't moving one bit.
This happens week after week after week.
The excitement you had when you first started an email list has fizzled out.
You know an email list is important, but if only it wasn't so difficult to actually send them something…
You're already pressed for time writing blog posts.
How do you manage fresh content for your email as well?
Sound familiar?"

Headline: 7 ridiculously simple reasons why your blog's not growing (and how to fix it)

Blog post Opener:

"I'm pretty sure you know the feeling.
This feeling of frustration to see some growth…
…ANY growth on your blog…
You feel like you've tried every possible strategy.…But things aren't moving as fast as you'd like.
You just don't seem to be getting the ROI for your efforts.
Forget money.
You're not even getting shares, subscribers, recognition or engagement.
If only you could get out of this deep rut you seem to have fallen into….
If only you knew why you weren't making as much progress.
I've been there too.
Struggling in the trenches to get my blog to where I want it to be.
To see some progress…any progress for that matter."

We'll discuss in further detail how to package your target audience's list of motivations, desires, and frustrations in your content in Section III.

Ask Who You Already Have Access To

If you already have clients and blog subscribers, ask them directly what their fears, aspirations and frustrations are. Keep your questions open-ended to encourage responses. I have a list of survey questions you can send in the bonus pack.

After doing a little work to identify your reader persona, you should be able to come up with a description like this:

Emily is a stay-at-home mother of two children under the age of six. She wants to earn some income on the side to help with the household expenses. Lately she has been toying with the idea of starting a blog and freelancing, but she's not sure if she has the time for it, especially with her kids.

She fears that she is not an expert on anything in particular and doesn't know what to write about. She never misses MarieTV episodes on Tuesdays and tries to learn as much as possible about writing from Carol Tice's website Make a Living Writing. She relies on Facebook to keep up with the latest news during her lunch hour.

Writing for Emily is so much easier than writing for an invisible audience interested in blogging, don't you think?

For now, have a go at this exercise. Doing this exercise will help you build loyalty and credibility because your readers will know you understand them, and they'll trust you enough to start taking action on your guidance.

"It's like you were reading my mind!"
"I really needed to hear that today."

"Thank you. This was perfect timing."
"I need to get started on this. Thanks for the reminder."

When you start to get comments like the ones above, you'll know you're on the right track with understanding your audience.

Action Item:

Create a detailed description of your target audience.

Chapter 3

VIEW YOUR CONTENT AS A LINCHPIN IN THE READER JOURNEY

You now have a better understanding of your ideal reader and how you're going to help them.

And there are various stages that an ideal reader goes through as they come into contact with your brand.

Here's what the typical journey is like for a reader:

Stranger › Casual reader › Subscriber › Engaged subscriber and fan › Brand advocate + Customer

Your content is the linchpin that moves the reader through these different stages. Matching the right content to where your audience is on their journey with you is critical to helping them move forward.

Stranger to Casual Reader

How do you get a stranger to become a casual reader? This person has absolutely no clue about you, so you need to promote yourself and your content on channels outside of your blog.

Social media is an obvious option.

But apart from that you could do guest posts, speak on podcasts and create slide shares. These are activities that will get readers onto your site. They will click through after engaging with a call to action in a Facebook promotion thread or an enticing headline on Pinterest. If your content exceeds expectations and keeps the promise of your headline, they become a reader.

Casual Reader to Subscriber

To convert a casual reader into a subscriber you need to offer a compelling lead magnet (or opt-in freebie as it's commonly known in blogging niches) that is too good to miss out on.

Subscriber to Engaged Subscriber and Fan

Many bloggers think their job is done as soon as someone gets on their email list, but the process doesn't stop there.

You still need to convert a subscriber into an *engaged* subscriber. You need to produce content that empowers and educates.

For instance, if you are helping people quit their jobs…as the very first step you can help *prepare* people to quit their jobs. You can give them a list of business ideas they can start quickly and on a budget to encourage them to quit their jobs. Remember we spoke about the Driver of Change (DoC) method in the previous chapter? By helping them with the first step, you are seeding the 'change' that you ultimately want to create for them. This is how you create engaged subscribers and eventually fans.

Engaged Subscriber and Fan to Brand Advocate and Customer

Now that you have engaged subscribers, how do you get them to become customers? How do you get them to buy from you? You do this by creating content that points in the direction of your products and services. You remove objections and create desire for your products and services. We'll see exactly how you can do this in Chapter 6.

Action Item:

Do you have any content gaps that hinder the journey from stranger to brand advocate and customer? Think about where your content is missing out on opportunities to inch your reader forward.

Chapter 4

POSITION YOUR BRAND AND CONTENT IN THE ONLINE SPACE

So far, you've taken a deep dive into the content categories (or buckets) of your blog and identified your ideal reader. You've also started to view your content as a critical factor in moving the reader forward.

It's important now to take a step back and think about your brand and content in the online space.

How different are you from the thousands of blogs in your niche and what do you want to be known for?

Look five years down the road.

What topic or content do you want to be associated with? What types of products and services do you see yourself offering. What type of business and community do you want to create?

These could form the core categories of your blog. When you repeatedly produce content on a few core categories, you get associated with those categories. You build authority and your blog becomes a go-to for those topics.

But building content authority comes with having a distinctive point of view.

For instance, I chose email marketing as a core category on my blog because I felt I had something different to say from what everyone else was saying. The blogging and marketing niche I was in was positioning huge email lists as an end to a successful business – a magic bullet – an elixir that could solve all problems. But no one was educating and empowering people on how they should be using their email list. I also saw lots of people struggling with not knowing what type of content to send their email list.

I knew I had a distinctive point of view and a message that was timely. I worked on publishing content pieces which displayed my distinctive point of view on this topic.

In Content Inc, Author Joe Puluzzi calls this the 'content tilt.' The content tilt is what will separate you from everyone else in your niche. The content tilt is what makes you and your content different. This is what will get your audience to take notice of you and reward you with their attention. There are a few ways you can find your own tilt.

- What questions are your audience members asking but aren't addressed in your niche?
- What perspectives and viewpoints in your niche do you oppose or take an opposite view on?
- What is everyone saying that isn't necessarily true.
- Do you disagree with any view point widely held in your niche?
- Are there any specific methods you use that get your readers/clients results?
- What are common misconceptions and mistakes readers have about the content in your niche?
- What are your biggest light bulb moments that have impacted the way you do certain things and how you help your readers or clients?

All of these are questions you can ask yourself to help you figure out your own 'content tilt.'

Now, you don't have to answer all of them. And if you do have several ideas, methods or thought processes that are different, think about which will have the biggest impact. Which are most aligned with the goals and vision you have for your blog and business? Which do you want to have your name associated with?

Once you've figured out what that is, use that as your brand footprint.

You want to burn in that point of view into almost every single touch point you have with your audience. This is what is going to help you position your brand in the crowded online space.

Action Item:

What's your own 'Content tilt'? What do you think you have a unique perspective in? How different is your content?

Take a deep breathe now. We're heading into the One-Hour Content Plan.

Section II

THE ONE-HOUR CONTENT PLAN

Here's what a blank template of the One-Hour Content Plan looks like.

There are four different parts to this plan.

And it's designed so you can fill it in as you read this book. You *will* know when to fill it in because I'll give you an action step when it's time to do so.

For now, download the templates.

Get acquainted with the way it looks.

And then determine how much content you will actually need for a full year. That depends on how frequently you plan to publish your content. Here's a guideline you can use so you know what you have to work with.

	6 Months	12 Months
Weekly	26	52
Twice a week	48	96
Once every 2 weeks	12	24

When you work on the content plan, do not put *any* effort into coming up with a good title. Your main goal at this stage is to generate ideas. You can refine and critique them later. If your headlines or titles look sloppy and you don't know exactly what you're going to say in that piece of content, that's perfectly ok.

Once you have filled out the One-Hour Content Plan, put your ideas together in an editorial calendar. We'll talk more about how to set-up an editorial calendar in section IV.

If you're looking for an editorial planner, I designed the CREATE Planner to complement this method of content planning. You can have a look at it here: CREATEPLANNER.COM

Category:

	Sub-Categories
1	
2	
3	
4	
5	
6	

Now you're ready to flesh out your blog post ideas. Copy the category and sub-category from the above page.

Pick one sub-category and break it down into blog post ideas.

Remember to ask yourself **"what does the reader need to know to be well-versed in this sub-category." Don't overthink the process. Your titles do not need to be refined at this stage. You can always refine and critique your ideas later.**

Repeat the process for each category and sub-category.

1	Blog post title !
2	
3	
4	
5	
6	

Name of Product

What core problem does the product solve?	Attention Posts	
What's the promise of your product?	Interest	
What does someone need to be aware of before purchasing your product?	Desire	

Name of Service	
What core problem does the service solve?	Attention Posts
What's the promise of your service?	Interest
What does someone need to be aware of before hiring you or engaging your service?	Desire

Section III

CONTENT IDEATION (COMING UP WITH CONTENT IDEAS)

In this section you will learn three different strategies or what I call the **E.O.G.** (Expert —Offer—Goal) Method of coming up with content ideas. We will then go to the granular level to look at the different types of posts you can write to feed your content plan.

Before we dive into ideation, you need a system to capture content ideas and content inspiration.

How you heard of the term swipe file?

A swipe file is filled with ideas that inspire you and that you'd like to explore further. If you aren't already keeping a file of ideas, start now.

A swipe file can be an email folder, physical file or app. A simple Google spreadsheet will also do the trick. Make a tab for each of your content categories within the spreadsheet to store ideas.

Trello and Evernote are other systems you can use.

No one method is better than the other. But the pressure of having to learn a tool should not deter or stop you from using a swipe file. Use a tool with the least friction and resistance and get started with it to house your content ideas.

But how do you *feed* that swipe file? You do this via research, and I'll give you a few different ways you can do so.

A quick note before we explore what these different ways are. You're not putting *any* interesting idea you come across into your swipe file. You're putting ideas that are aligned with your content GPS - what we defined in Section I.

1. Pinterest

One of my favorite ways to search for ideas and swipe them at the same time is Pinterest. If you come across a pin image with an interesting title, click save and pin it to a secret board. You can create a board to store blog post ideas and make it a secret board so that no one is able to see it.

2. Facebook Groups

Facebook groups are a wealth of information especially if your target audience hang out there. Use the "Search this group" box and type in your keywords (preserving the quotes) to instantly see the type of questions they are asking.

3. Buzzsumo

Use this tool to search a keyword or domain to get a breakdown of the most popular content in terms of social shares for the site. This will give you an idea of what type of content is popular or even going viral in that space as well as the comments readers are leaving.

4. iTunes

Podcasts are really popular and there is almost definitely a podcast (or many) on the topic you are looking for. Do a search within iTunes for the keyword and filter to view the most popular episodes first. Once you find an episode that looks promising, search for the show notes and have a look at the angle and points mentioned. Use this as a pivot for your own ideas.

5. Answer the Public

This shows you what questions people are asking about your topic. Enter your keyword, select your country, and then the tool will display various types of questions that people are typing into Google for that keyword.

6. Soovle

Soovle gives you a quick snapshot of the most popular searches in Amazon, Bing, Youtube, Answer.com, Yahoo and Wikipedia based on your keyword.

7. Ubersuggest

Ubersuggest helps you quickly find several new keyword ideas based on your original search.

8. Competitors

Are there bloggers in your space that are bigger than you? Look at the content that's popular on their site. Use Buzzsumo to find out what their top posts are. Look at the comments on their posts to determine what your target audience are looking for.

Before you consider attempting a piece of content that has already done well for someone else, ask yourself two questions:

1. Will your content add to the conversation that's already out there?

Have a look at your niche. Has this been said before? Will this piece make a contribution to the existing content on this topic?

2. If you think it's better, in what way?

You can add value to an existing piece of content in three different ways.

- You take an opposing view on it and go against the grain.
- You take a different angle or perspective that the author has not considered.
- You add to the content because it's not complete.

Not every piece of content is going to be a masterpiece. And there could be thousands of people who have already written about your topic. But set out to make every piece of content exceptional because when you do, people will start to notice and share your work in Facebook groups and other social media platforms without you even asking. The more people share, the more traffic you get.

Now that you have a better idea of how to feed your swipe file, let's get started on how to come up with blog post content ideas using the **E.O.G.** (Expert –Offer–Goal) **Method**.

Action Item:

Choose a storage system for your swipe file. There's no right or wrong answer – only what works for you.

Chapter 5

HOW TO BUILD CONTENT AROUND TOPICS THAT ARE RELEVANT TO YOUR BLOG'S PURPOSE

We spoke about your blog purpose and your main content buckets in Section I of this book. In this chapter we'll discuss how to break down your categories into sub-categories and blog posts.

I call this the **'Expert'** method because you're creating content so that the reader becomes 'well versed' or 'proficient' in this category.

There isn't any way your reader can be a master of a particular category of content through a single blog post or piece of content. A few different pieces of content have to come together to help your reader grasp a particular category. This is where your sub-categories come in handy.

Like I mentioned earlier, email marketing is a core category on my blog.

To pick out my sub-categories, I ask myself **"what does the reader need to know to become proficient in this category?"** I then list sub-categories such as:

- Email list growth
- Nurturing subscribers
- Running re-engagement campaigns
- How to create lead magnets
- How to create landing pages
- Tools for list growth
- How to optimize conversions

I would then break each sub-category into topics (blog posts).

Let's take a website for moms who are attempting to build a home VA business. The categories could be:

- Marketing yourself
- Dealing with clients
- Pricing your services

Let's just work with one category right now. Let's break up the 'Marketing' category into Category › Sub-Category › Blog posts

Category - Marketing yourself
I have two sub-categories at this moment:

1. How to write a pitch
2. How to have a good writer website

Let's break each of these sub-categories down.

Sub-category 1 : How to write a pitch

Blog Posts:

- Should you cold pitch your VA services?
- 20 essential elements that make a killer pitch
- The perfect VA pitch template: What clients look out for before hiring
- How to go from pitch to contract in 5 simple steps
- 20 mistakes you make when you pitch a client
- Cold vs Warm Pitches. Which is better?
- 10 types of testimonials you need to have before pitching a high net worth client

Sub-category 2: How to have a good writer website

Blog Posts:

- 5 Essential components of a freelance writer website
- Is your website leaking potential leads and clients?
- 10 authority boosting elements to add on your freelance writer homepage
- 5 different types of content you need to attract your dream client

- 10 tell tale signs your website needs a makeover

Did you see what we just did there?

You can expand and dive deeper into each of your categories and sub-categories. This system will give you an endless list of blog post ideas to work with at any one time even if you have no products or services.

Action Item:

Head to the One-Hour Content Plan. Fill out the first two pages. Need extra worksheets? I have bonus worksheets you can download at 1HCP.ME/BONUS

Chapter 6

CONTENT IDEAS TO PROMOTE YOUR PRODUCT AND SERVICE OFFERS

Before we dive deep into this chapter, you need to understand that people who experience your content will fall into one of five categories. Once you understand this concept, you're going to find it easy to create content around your products and services.

Let's dive in to the **'Offer'** method of content ideation.

Category 1: They have no idea about the problem that your product or service solves.

Some of them may not even be aware of the problem your product solves or why it needs to be solved in the first place.

Type of content for this category: Your content has to bring attention to the problem. Pain is more effective than stating the benefits. Dig into the pain of what they are going through.

Examples of post types for this category:

X _____ you didn't know about_____
E.g. 12 things you didn't know about heart disease / 10 things you didn't know about working from home

Why you should stop _____
E.g. Why you should stop sending blog post notifications / why you should stop writing about your children / why you should stop private Twitter DMs

Why your _____ sucks and what to do about it
E.g. Why your resume sucks... / why your DIY blog sucks / why your webinar sucks...

X _____ sins and what to do to rectify them
E.g. 7 email marketing sins.. / 10 parenting sins..

X mistakes [call out an audience] make on their _____
E.g. 12 mistakes mom bloggers make with their media kits / 7 mistakes college graduates make on their resumes

X reasons your _____ will fail
E.g. 10 reasons your VA business will fail

Category 2: They are starting to become aware of the problem that your product or service solves. They still have a lot of questions, but you've got their attention and they are starting to trust you.

Type of content for this category: These are posts that are going to maintain people's interest once they're at your blog or on your list. For example, if an attention grabbing post tells them the seven mistakes they might be making in your niche, then the interest post shows them how to avoid those mistakes.

Examples of post types for this category:

9 ridiculously simple shortcuts to _____ (make turkey / cut chicken / write a book...the possibilities are endless)

The lazy _____ guide to _____
E.g. The lazy parent's guide to making dinner / The lazy marketer's guide to selling / The lazy blogger's guide to writing long-form content

X evergreen ideas for _____
This can be anything from a dinner party / birthday party / social media updates / blog posts

How to create a _____ and follow it
E.g. How to create a writing habit and follow it / how to create a marketing strategy and follow it

Have a _____ you can be proud of
E.g. Have a body / clientele / home organization routine / work schedule you can be proud of

A skill every [call out an audience] should have and why

Category 3: They are aware of the problem that your product or service solves. They trust you and love your content. Often, they feel the product is right for them but they're not quite ready to buy.

Here's what one of my subscribers Karen said, "Hi Meera! Your course looks so fabulous but, for me, I think it's too much too soon.

I started to work on my self-hosted blog in November/December 2015. I probably should have just paid someone to set up my blog for me because it's waaaay more complicated than I thought it would be, terribly frustrating, and it's still not ready. Next thing I need to do is just get the welcome email campaign ready to go. Heck, I'm just figuring out what a Landing Page is!

Thanks for the emails... one of these days I'll be ready to take another step!"

Type of content for this category: Case studies of your students or clients or even of yourself are great for this category. You can also write a post highlighting your own experience or asking them to imagine how different their life would be with your product. The content has to instill desire for your product or service.

Examples of post types for this category

Talk about the best business/blog investment you made and why. Explain how and why that investment helped you.

X questions you need to ask before signing up for [affiliate product category]
E.g. 5 questions you need to ask before signing for a email marketing service/landing pages software/stock photo site. Explain why they need to consider these five questions and then showcase how your affiliate product can help address that need or problem.

Why I hate _____
E.g. Why I hate designing blog images / Why I hate email marketing / Why I hate traveling with the kids. List your reasons and then talk about how your product has helped you. This will work great for email and a blog post.

X reasons you need to be using [affiliate product category]

Category 4: They are ready to buy but they have questions.

I received the following message from Alex, one of my subscribers on my Facebook page:

Alex: Does this help a product based business, not just digital?

Me: If you're collecting leads online for that product business then definitely. You can nurture them via email and direct them to your physical store or product.

Alex: Thanks! Just a bit nervous I won't see ROI.

Me: Have you taken the free email course yet? You could start with that first.

Alex: No no, I've read your blog and it's great content. I just need to dive in and be done. I've talked to someone who's been in your course.

Me: Ok awesome! You can always come back to me if you need some tailored help with how to use it for your particular situation.

Alex: Thank you! I appreciate it.

The entire conversation took ten minutes max and she purchased less than ten minutes later. These people are ready to buy and need an incentive or some guidance and encouragement and you have the sale. You have to be present, willing and patient to take their questions.

Type of content for this category: Have a detailed FAQ section on your sales page. Install a free live chat function like Drift or Tawk.to on your sales page. Reply to any emails in a timely fashion. Your content has to highlight the benefits of your solution to inspire action.

5. They've purchased. They are ready for more good stuff from you.

Have an on-boarding or email series that introduces them to your product and holds their hand through the process.

Now, all these content pieces aren't necessarily in a series of blog posts. They could also follow through over email or video.

To effectively move your readers from one phase to another, answer the following question:

"What keeps my audience stuck in this phase and what do they need from me and my content to move forward?"

Let's take a look at how to put this into practice with real life examples.

I have a course called Email Lists Simplified.

Core problem that my course solves: Don't know what emails to send their subscribers. Don't know how to write a welcome email series.

Solution the course provides: Helps bloggers and solopreneurs create a strategy and plan for their email list.

What does someone need to know <u>before</u> being ready to purchase my course: Why email isn't just about growing your list. Why nurturing your email list is important. The need to send regular emails to your list.

If you have a look at my blog content on this category, every piece of content acts as a long form sales letter for my course Email Lists Simplified. It prepares the reader to purchase the course.

Let's take another example of Vanessa, one of my readers who wants to sell an ebook about what it takes to form new habits and break old ones.

Core problem that the ebook addresses: Unable to break old habits

Solution the ebook provides: Ebook helps you take small steps to break old habits in 30 days

What does someone need to know <u>before</u> being ready to purchase the ebook: There is a simple strategy to break old habits. Why mindset is the biggest stumbling block.

Here are examples of content pieces she can create.

1. Why it's so difficult to break old habits or create new ones (Bringing attention to the problem)
2. December dread. The cost of not taking action (Bringing attention to the problem)

3. Mistakes people make with starting a new project and why you're doomed to fail before even starting (Bringing attention to the problem)
4. 10 mindset issues you need to fix before forming a new habit (Brings interest to the solution)
5. How you or your client or student changed their life around with a 30-day roadmap (Desire)
6. What it takes to create a new habit and how you can start today (Create desire for your ebook)

Let's take another example of Patricia, a VA who was finding it difficult to find clients.

Here are the questions someone has or needs to know before hiring her:

- What types of tasks to outsource
- What's the right price point?
- Where to find good VAs
- How to pick the right one?

Here are examples of content pieces she can create.

1. 10 red flags you should look out for in hiring a VA (Bring attention to problem so that they will know that she could be a safe alternative)
2. Why the DIY way could cost you thousands of dollars in wasted opportunity (Bring attention to problem)

3. The cost of not focusing on your growth tasks (Bring attention to problem)
4. What tasks can you outsource to your VA? (Interest)
5. Working with a VA? 20 things you need to discuss beforehand (Interest)
6. What a match made in VA heaven looks like (Create desire for your solution - Hiring YOU)

Having strategic content pieces like these will help you boost your product and service sales.

If you're having a launch for a service or product or if you're an affiliate for a course that goes on sale, you can map out your pieces of content in this way to prime your audience for the sale.

Action Item:

Have an offer or service? Fill out the last two sections of the content plan. Build yourself a calendar of events that are important to your niche and business (launches, sales etc). Work back on the content pieces you need to prime your audience for those events.

Chapter 7

GOAL AND CONTENT: A RECIPE FOR SUCCESS

This method of coming up with content ideas is dependent on your goals.

Determine your goals for the quarter.

Here's an example:

Quarter 1 Goals

1. Increase email list to 500 subscribers
2. Make first $200-$500

Here's how your goals will determine your content direction.

Content based on Goal 1

- I will make an additional opt-in incentive
- I will guest post on four blogs by the end of the quarter

Content based on Goal 2

- I will write two detailed tutorials on my chosen affiliate product
- I will make a bonus ebook for subscribers who purchase through my affiliate link

When you create content that's closely tied to your goals, every piece of content has purpose and you know exactly how it's going to help you attain your goals.

The type of method you choose to create ideas will depend on the stage you're at with your blog and business.

If you have no products and services yet, the 'Expert' and 'Goal' methods will work for you. If you already have a suite of products and services or ones that you're an affiliate for, then you can combine the methods above to come up with content ideas.

Now you know the different methods of coming up with content ideas. Here's where we talk about the different types of posts and how they might fit into your content plan.

Action Item:

Set quarterly goals and determine what content pieces will help you achieve it.

Chapter 8

DIFFERENT TYPES OF POSTS TO FEED YOUR CONTENT IDEAS

You now know different methods of coming up with content ideas. Here are 10 different types of posts to feed each of these content ideas.

Myths/Pick a fight

Perfect for: Establishing your leadership or bringing attention to a topic.

These are posts that reflect your view point and break down widely held beliefs in your niche and industry. If you disagree with a certain view point in your niche and if there are common mistakes and misconceptions that you see several clients and customers making and having, this is a good type of post to write.

If there are any overused phrases or angles in your niche that you can take an opposing view on, this is also a good type of post to express your thought leadership. For instance, to me this would be phrases like 'the money is in the list' or 'the bigger the list the better'.

Examples

X things the experts don't tell you about _____
E.g. 12 things the experts don't tell you about blogging / 6 things the experts don't tell you about organic food

X myths about _____ that you need to steer clear from
E.g. 5 myths about blogging / going on a paleo lifestyle / losing pregnancy weight / using Pinterest

What the best _____ know about ____that you don't
E.g. What the best bloggers know about email marketing that you don't / what the best writers know about using writing software that you don't / what the best teachers know about free play that you don't

Choose a myth that several people in your industry believe in and prove them wrong with evidence and research.

E.g. Breakfast is the most important meal in the day.

Guides or Ultimate Posts

Perfect for: Establishing expertise in your topic and raising interest in the topic.

Examples

The rebel's guide to _____

The bootstrapper's guide to _____(website design / wholesale / guerrilla marketing ideas / dieting)

Mistakes

Perfect for: Bringing attention to a topic. Getting your readers to sit up and take notice

Examples

Why you should stop _____
E.g. Why you should stop sending blog post notifications / why you should stop writing about your children / why you should stop private twitter DMs

Why your _____ sucks and what to do about it
E.g. Why your resume sucks / why your DIY blog sucks / why your webinar sucks

X _____ sins and what to do to rectify them
E.g. 7 email marketing sins / 10 parenting sins

X mistakes [call out an audience] make on their _____
E.g. 12 mistakes mom bloggers make with their media kits / 7 mistakes college graduates make on their resumes

X reasons your _ _ _ _ _ will fail

E.g 5 reasons your blog will fail / 5 reasons your weight loss diet will fail

Trends

Perfect for: Establishing authority and thought leadership.

Write about a trend you notice and your prediction about it.

This doesn't have to be something earth shockingly major. Remember when many female entrepreneurs started using gold in their website color palettes? If you're a website designer, write about what you feel about that trend and if it's still relevant now.

Likewise, are there topics in your niche that everyone suddenly seems to be talking about?

Where do you see yourself in five years?

If you're blogging, you must satisfy a need or a problem. Maybe you're helping other women get in touch with their spiritual side or you want to revolutionize elementary teaching. Set goals and paint a picture of the next five years. Encourage your readers and subscribers to look ahead as well.

Examples

Why this is the perfect time to jump on _ _ _ _ _ _

Considering _ _ _ _ for your business? 5 questions to think about

Is _ _ _ _ _ right for you? Here's where I see _ _ _ _ _ in 5 years.

Curated content/Roundup posts

Perfect for: Raising attention and awareness. Many new bloggers post curated content pieces to drive traffic.

This is where you curate popular pieces of content on a focused topic from other influencers and people in your niche. These posts typically attract a lot of attention because it brings together lots of influencers who may have huge social media followings. Here's an example of one such post by Erika Madden of Olyvia.Co: http://olyvia.co/helpful-blog-posts-to-make-you-better-blogger/

The roundup post featuring quotes from others in your niche is another type of content that attracts a lot of attention.

Examples

X top blog posts about _ _ _ _ _ _

E.g. 20 top blog posts about landing pages / 10 top blog posts about under 30 minute recipes

X _____ every [call out an audience] needs to be [ACTION]

E.g. 10 email lists every social media manager needs to be subscribed to / 10 books every aspiring entrepreneur in his forties needs to be reading.

Best _____ from X experts

E.g. Best examples of email headlines from 20 experts / Best productivity tips from 10 experts

How X _____ do _____

E.g. How 5 social media managers automate their updates / How 10 food bloggers take their photography

X _____ tips from X ____

E.g. 50 photography tips from DIY bloggers / 30 website design tips from 10 developers

Case studies

Perfect for: Creating desire for your call to action.

Case studies break down a specific topic and dive deep into it to show outcomes, both good and bad. A case study is a good post type to use especially if you are showcasing your results with a particular tool or course that you may be an affiliate for. It's also good to utilize case studies to showcase results students and clients have had using your products and methods.

When you present case studies, be sure to give tangible takeaways and how readers can apply it to their own situations.

Success and failures

Perfect for: Bringing attention to a topic. Getting your readers to sit up and take notice.

Examples

Write about what you would have done differently for your blog, website or business if you could start over.

Tell them about a missed opportunity. Take this as a chance to inspire and motivate your subscribers and readers. Show them your vulnerable side and let them connect with you.

Share about a terrible job or client you had. What has that taught you and how does it affect how you do things now?

Why I _____ when I had _____

E.g. Why I invested in Convertkit when I was earning $0 on my blog

Useful Tools or Services

Examples

X time saving services for small business in [call out your niche]

How to save yourself a few hours every week with (technique/tool/product)
E.g. How to save yourself a few hours every week with IFFFT / Buffer / Pomodoro / freezer meals

When NOT to use _____
E.g. When not to use Wordpress / tool / technique such as Pomodoro or GTD

Creative ways to use_____
E.g. Creative ways to use leftover chicken / broccoli stalks / Tweepi / Follerwonk / Outreach Ninja (any tool would fit in here)

Questions

Perfect for: Raising interest in the topic.

You can write a post to address a popular question you always get asked or you see being asked regularly in your niche. You could also pool popular questions together and address them in a post.

Interviews

Perfect for: Bringing desire for your call to action.

Share a video interview with a subscriber / customer / client who got results by implementing your strategy or tip.

Section IV

THE PERFECT CONTENT PACKAGE

You've defined your content playing field.

You know different methods of coming up with content ideas. You've also saved yourself a massive amount of time by coming up with a good six to twelve months worth of content ideas – all in one go.

But your plan is only fully functional if your content has three critical elements. Your content has to attract, delight and convert your readers. Add these three elements to the implementation of your content plan, and you'll have a fully functioning blog content strategy.

In this section we'll start by addressing what it means to package your content in a way that attracts the attention of your target audience. You'll discover a simple strategy to know exactly what it means to write in your 'brand voice.' You'll also find tips on how to optimize each of the eight parts of your content so that Google and your readers love it.

As Randi Zuckerberg writes in her book, Dot Complicated, attention comes at a premium in our wired world. Attention is currency. The right content package accentuates and contributes to the flavor of your content.

Chapter 9

INJECT CONTENT WITH A POWERFUL BRAND VOICE

Like it or not, if you're publishing content you already have a brand voice.

Whether that's the brand voice you intentionally chose, or something you want or even like are questions you need to consider.

A brand voice is the tone you use to communicate with your audience.

The words, tone and style you use in your writing say a lot about your brand. And each and every one of us has a personal brand whether we see ourselves as a blogger, solopreneur or a small business owner. This is why you don't ever want to leave defining your brand voice to chance.

A brand voice should be consistent across your content pieces. If you're not careful, you can end up with a random concoction of voices and tones in the content you produce across different platforms. This doesn't provide a consistent picture of your brand and you become wishy washy. You start attracting disparate segments of people and end up confusing your target audience as a result.

This inconsistent experience is what you don't want. You also don't want to sound like others in your niche.

Here's what Jason Fried, founder of Basecamp says, "When you write like everyone else, you're saying, 'Our products are like everyone else's.' Would you go to a dinner party and repeat what the person to the right of you is saying all night long? Would that be interesting to anybody? Why are so many businesses saying the same things at the biggest party on the planet — the marketplace?"

Here are three steps you can take to define your brand voice.

1. Take stock.
Have a look at your current content. Which content pieces have a similar tone across them. Which ones are unique to your style. Which ones sound like they could be written by someone else in your niche.

2. What words describe your brand?
If your brand was a person how would you describe him or her?

Pick three attribute words to describe your brand. Is your brand funny, warm, girly or quirky? Or is it sophisticated, modern and serious?

Here are some examples of attribute words you can use.

The words you've identified with your brand will also influence your writing voice. There are no right or wrong answers to these — just what's right for your brand and the target audience you identified in the first section.

Analytical	Artistic	Authentic
Authoritative	Bold	Bright
Caring	Candid	Charming
Clear	Calm	Colorful
Cheerful	Chic	Compassionate
Daring	Dangerous	Detailed
Daring	Dynamic	Delightful
Elegant	Edgy	Energetic
Exciting	Fun	Frank
Feminine	Flirty	Girly
Genuine	Humorous	Honest

Intense	Inspiring	Informal
Kind	Knowledgeable	Motivating
Outspoken	Out of the box	Over-deliver
Optimistic	Professional	Powerful
Playful	Rebellious	Smart
Spiritual	Strong	Stylish
Simple	Sophisticated	Silly
Strong	Trustworthy	Thoughtful
Quirky	Upbeat	Unique
Whimsical	Warm	Witty

Now that you have identified three words, qualify what these aren't. For instance, your brand is bold but not arrogant. Fun but not wishy-washy. Honest but not hurtful. These will give you a set of markers that identify your brand voice.

If you have an existing audience, what words are you able to pick out from their comments and feedback? Is there alignment in how you describe your brand and they do? This gives you clues as to how you need to pivot.

3. Put these together using the ADDE (Attribute Markers - Do's - Dont's - Expressions) Formula

Do's are a short description of what your attribute markers actually mean. Don'ts define how you don't want your brand voice to come across. And the expressions drill down into the tiny nuances of how your brand voice comes across.

Attribute Markers	Do's	Don'ts	Special expressions
Honest but not hurtful.	Honest about mistakes and failures. Keep promises and pride customer service. Reply personally to emails	Oversell or hardsell. Push what they are losing out by not purchasing your product	Use emojis like :) in writing

Bold but not arrogant.	Not afraid to challenge status quo viewpoints in the niche. Never apologize for contrarian standpoint.	Use jargon. Use expletives.Use passive voice	Talk soon, Say WHAAT
Fun but not wishy-washy	Expressive. Use names to call your tribe and don't apologize for it.	Use expletives. Use passive voice.	Sign off with xoxo

Now that you've defined your voice and tone, go a step further and add in special expressions that embellish your writing.

- Do you use slang or expressive phrases, such as "Hey lovelies!", "Say WHHAAT?" or "Hi Buttercup"?
- Do you use emojis in your writing?
- Do you start sentences with conjunctions such as and? Do you end your posts or emails in a certain way? (i.e. *XOXO, Hugs, till later, talk soon*)
- Do you use CAPS or italics for emphasis?

- Do you use acronyms in your writing? (i.e. LOL, ROFL, LMAO)

Action Item:

Determine your brand voice by filling out the ADDE table. Download a template at 1HCP.ME/BONUS

Chapter 10

WHAT IS THE BEST CONTENT FORMAT?

This is what you hear:

- Why aren't you doing more videos? Video is how you need to be building your audience.
- Webinars are the holy grail of marketing.
- YouTube is the second largest search engine and you need to be there to grow your business.

I'm going to go against the grain in telling you this next thing.

There's no point in indulging in a content format that keeps you locked in a room for hours crying while trying to create. The more you create content in the format that's your strength, the more you attract your target audience.

That's one of the reasons I don't do video with regularity. I can write and that's where I'm my best. I will definitely lose the audience that loves video, but I'd rather attract an audience that aligns with the format I'm most comfortable with and is in my zone of genius. You can't be for everyone, and that's ok.

Here's what Lacy Boggs, Founder of the Content Direction Agency said about her experiment with Podcasts and why they decided to call it quits, "…those download numbers were just a vanity metric in this case. We weren't seeing any real movement for our businesses: no one was seeing an increase in opt-ins, and definitely none of us was making any money yet. But we had collectively paid thousands of dollars to make this happen, not to mention our time.

It started to become more work than it was worth. And, after about nine months, we cancelled the experiment. Objectively, this attempt at innovation in our content marketing failed."

Pick a format that you enjoy creating content in, moves you closer to your goals, gives you measurable results and that you can consistently produce. Get consistent in one content format *before* choosing to add another.

Does this channel provide a better way for your audience to understand this topic or experience something that text alone can't offer?

If you can't answer yes, rethink whether it is the best format for your content. Don't be afraid to say no.

In the next chapter we'll get into the nitty gritty of how to write your blog post so that it's optimized for both the search engines and your readers' experience.

Chapter 11

HOW TO CREATE SMART BLOG POSTS THAT KEEP READERS HOOKED

'We need more content', said no one.

There are about 2 million blog posts published every single day. There isn't a dearth of quality content out there. Your readers are being pulled in thousands of different directions.

Your blog posts can be dripping with value but still get no readers. It could be well researched and annotated with references and it'll still not make a difference. Here's an email I received from one of my clients.

"Meera, I think I write pretty well. But I still don't get shares on my blog posts. Every post I publish is a struggle."

Sound familiar?

If you're serious about standing out, your content has to disrupt their attention, draw them in by empathizing and compel them to opt-in to your email list to continue where the blog post has ended.

The problem possibly lies with the way you've structured your blog posts.

In this chapter I'll walk you through eight different components that will give your blog post an uplift and shine.

Embellish your content with these eight components and when your post is publish-ready, it'll hook your audience and get them reading until the end.

1. The Headline
Your headline sells your blog post. It determines whether your site gets a click-through or not from social media. Your headline is a constant work in progress and you should never use the first headline you come up with.

Here are a few elements that are critical to a winning headline.

Be clear first, clever second.
You don't want to be clever with your headline at the expense of clarity. Your headline should convey one main idea and your reader should be clear within a couple of seconds about what you want them to achieve or obtain from your post.

Examples:

How You Can [desired result] Almost Instantly

The Quickest & Easiest Way To [desired result]

Increase Your [desired result] In [time period]

Be specific in your headline.

Use numbers, minutes, hours, days and percentages to communicate and accentuate the benefit or promise of the post.

Examples:

Take X minutes to get started with [blank]

X Questions Answered About [blank]

How I got X subscribers in [time period]

Address a specific emotion such as fear of losing out, wanting to achieve happiness, fear of failure, wanting results, wanting to be loved or liked.

Examples:

Do You Recognize the [number] Early Warning Signs of [blank]?

X Shocking Mistakes Killing Your [blank]

[Blank] May Be Causing You To Lose Out On [desired result]

Be sure your headline is searchable.

If your post is never found, then what's the point of writing exceptional content. Include keywords in your headline. A quick tip: Ask yourself if this headline is something that your reader would type into Google.If your answer is yes, then bingo, you've got a great headline.

2. Introduction

Your introduction includes a hook.

A hook is a compelling statement or paragraph in the introduction of your blog post. It grabs the reader's attention and urges them to keep reading.

Here are four examples of hooks you can use:

Ask your reader a direct question.

Example: What if you had 10 extra hours a day? How would that work for you? Would you spend more time with your family? Write a book?

Include a shocking statistic.

Examples: Did you know that 80% of daily blog visitors are new?

Did you know that once you accumulate 51 posts, blog traffic increases by 53%?

Showcase a benefit or an end result.

Examples: Imagine having 100,000 daily pageviews.

Imagine clicking send and seeing the sales pour in.

Add a Cliffhanger.
This is the opening Derek Halpern uses in his post These 5 little words can help you achieve anything. here's why…: "Yes. Just 5 little words can help you achieve anything. I'll explain…"

It makes you want to continue to read.

Another example is how Jeff Goins does it in his post I Got Everything I Wanted This Year (and It Wasn't as Thrilling as I Thought): "In 2015, I made more money than I've ever made before, grew my blog email list to over 100,000 people and published a best-selling book. So why at the end of the year did I still feel like I was missing something?"

3. Body of the blog post

Your subheads pique interest.
You're guilty of neglecting your subheads right? So am I.

But your subhead is what pulls your reader through the length of your blog posts. Once you've written your blog post, isolate your subheads and and see how they fare against these four elements: Curiosity, surprise, personality and emotion.

Use YOU instead of 'we' and 'I' in your writing.
Copyblogger's Brian Clark calls 'YOU' one of the most important words in blogging.

Writing with 'you' focuses on the reader. The reader is engaged. The reader has a reason to stick through the length of your posts because you are writing for her. The reader starts to trust that you care.

Here's what a little shift in perspective does:

"I'm having a bad day. I had a fight with my husband in the morning. My boss screamed at me. I needed to work late to finish a presentation, that too on my kid's birthday. Nothing is going right in my life. It's frustrating. It's unfair. I bet you feel that way too. So, here's where I can help."

Now change it up and use YOU.

"You're having a bad day. You had a fight with your husband in the morning. Your boss screamed at you. You need to work late to finish a presentation, that too on your kid's birthday. Nothing is going right in your life. It's frustrating. It's unfair. You deserve better, and I'm here to help."

See how a simple change of words creates a powerful picture? It allows you to slip into the skin of your target audience. It's a slice of your audience's life and if you get this right, you build connection and trust.

Include trigger words in your body.
Yes, you want to instantly turn your words into persuasive copy.

Yes, you want your blog posts to help, inspire and move your readers.

Yes, you want to get more engagement.

But how do you do it?

How do you connect with your readers when thousands of blogs clamor for their attention?

By including trigger words in your writing.

Smart Blogger outlines these trigger words in their article 17 Trigger Words That Work Like Cheat Codes for Getting Your Content Read

And 'Yes' is one of them. It pulls the reader along and persuades them to read on. These are other triggers words mentioned in the article: *You, Their Name, Because, Yes, Win, Stop, How, Instantly, Today, Everyone,Want, Easy, Discover, If, Worse, P.S. (Postscript)*

Be strategic. Place them in your headlines and lead your blog posts with them.

Break the English class rules—Use contractions.
Contractions keep your writing conversational and makes your writing engaging.

Do you not want to connect with your reader? vs Don't you want to connect with your reader?

This is not a fail-proof strategy. vs This isn't a fail-proof strategy.

It is amazing how a simple tweak can turn your writing around. vs It's amazing how a simple tweak can turn your writing around.

See the difference?

Have you asked questions?
Questions engage your reader. Ask the right questions and your reader nods and agrees with you. Social media examiner always start their blog posts with two questions.

Don't use passive voice.
'I appreciate your email' is better than 'Your email is much appreciated.'

Plug your writing into Hemingway app —a free web tool. The tool scans your writing and highlights adverbs, passive voice and complex sentences.

Take it with a grain of salt. Over editing using the app's recommendation might skew your writing voice, and that's the last thing you want.

Have you included links or screenshots to back-up your claims?
Yes, it takes longer to complete your posts. But the added time will pay off. You borrow authority by linking to influencers' links and research.

4. Format your post for scanners

How often have you clicked out of a site because of thick, dense, blocks of texts?

According to The Nielsen Norman Group, most visitors stick around for a mere 10-20 seconds before leaving. It also says that "people rarely read Web pages word by word; instead, they scan the page, picking out individual words and sentences."

A scanner protected post:

- Includes sub-heads every 3-4 paragraphs
- Keeps paragraphs no more than 3-4 sentences long
- Is generous with bullet points

Your blog post follows your content style guide.

One of the mistakes online entrepreneurs make is not having a content style guide. Are your headlines and subheads presented in the same way across your blog? Are you consistent with the way you present your numbers (one or 1)?

These are minor things which add up to the whole brand experience.

Interlink to older posts that are relevant.

When you start to blog for some time, you can lose track of your older content.

You need to put in place a system to capture your old content and keywords that go with each article. A simple spreadsheet like this will help.

Title of Post	Link	Keywords	Date published

This way, any time you feature a keyword in your writing, you can reference back to your spreadsheet to get the link. None of your old content will slip through the cracks again.

5. Conclusion

Your conclusion has to inspire your readers and encourage them to take action.
Your readers are probably feeling overwhelmed, lost and intimidated especially if you've written a long list post or a technical how-to post.

Here's what you can do to inspire and ease their woes in four quick steps:

- Remind them of the first step they can take.

- Give them confidence to implement two to three tips at a time.
- Nudge them to your content upgrade if it makes it easy to implement the steps.
- Show them how amazing the end result can be.

See how Neil Patel at the Quick Sprout blog does it with his post Want a 150% Boost in Traffic? Then Use This Idiot-Proof Guide to Google Authorship Markup.

He reminds the reader of the benefit of going through the technical steps in his post. He gives them confidence by telling them it'll take five to ten minutes to implement the steps. "…I believe if you take the time to go through these steps, you can have Google's authorship markup implemented within five to ten minutes. Sure, the results will take much longer, but I guarantee that you will not be disappointed with them!"

Make your last few sentences memorable.
Memorable sentences rhyme and use the power of three. Our brains understand, process and remember things better in three's.

Here are some examples: Just do it, Ready. Set. Go!, Blood, sweat and tears, Past, present and future.

Henneke Duistermaat at Enchanted Marketing uses the rule of 3 in her post: Why Adverbs Stink (and the Magic of Editing).

"Good writers aren't sprinters. They choose each and every word with care. They know the rules. But that also know how to break rules. Deliberately. Determinedly. Emphatically.

And in her post: 5 Persuasive Writing Tips: How to Write Mesmerizing Sales Copy Like Apple

"You need to understand what makes your readers tick. Appeal to their desires. Their wishes. Their dreams."

Include a call to action.

What do you want your readers to do and what's the goal of your content?

- Download your content upgrade?
- Make a comment?
- Share your article?

Adjust your call-to-action based on the goals of the post and state it at the end of the post.

Keep your conclusion to 200 words or less.

Your conclusion shouldn't include any new point or information. It closes the loop, inspires and is short. Try to keep your conclusion to about three paragraphs or 200 words.

6. Visuals

Your image is synchronous with your brand.

Your image has to be aligned with the same attributes that you defined for your brand. You can serve female entrepreneurs for instance and not use pink, gold or flowers because they're not aligned with the tone and voice of your brand.

Your social media visuals should follow a certain theme or mood.

These are some of my Pinterest images. Notice how they have a consistent visual theme?

As you start to get consistent with your social media images, your audience will start to recognize and pick them out as being *from you.*

Make your images SEO friendly.

Pictures should include the keyword in the title, alt tag, and filename.

Before uploading any pictures, change the filename of the image to match the keyword, rather than have something like d5673456.jpg.

7. Sticky Assets

Make sharing your posts easy.

If you want your readers to share your content, you have to make it easy for them to do so.

Click to tweets are great way to do this. Add three to seven click-to-tweets within each blog post.

You just have to head to the Click-to-tweet site, pre-write a tweet you'd like your readers to use. Generate a link. Add a button or 'tweet this' with the link on your blog posts. Or simply use the Better Click To Tweet plugin on Wordpress. All your readers have to do is click the "tweet" button to share it.

Add related posts.

You want your readers to stick around, click and keep reading. The more time they spend on your blog, the more likely they are to sign-up to your email list. Add related posts at the bottom of your blog posts to serve up relevant content. Use a related post plugin like Jetpack, Related Posts by Zemanta or Upprev.

8. Optimize Your Post for Search Engines

Include your top keyword in your Title tag.

Try to limit it to 55-65 characters. Your Title tag should stimulate your user's interest and make a promise. Limit these to 55-65 characters so they're not cut off when shown on search results.

Try to use different H1 and Title tags. Supplement your H1 tag with relevant keywords in order to get even more traffic.

Write a Meta Description of up to 130 characters.

Be sure to add a call to action, one to two keywords and relevant phrases in your meta description. Your meta description is the short snippet of your post that people see when it is listed among Google's search results. The easiest way to customize your **meta description** is by using the YOAST SEO Tool.

If you have the Yoast SEO plugin installed, you will see a box of options underneath your post in WordPress. To change the meta description, simply press "Edit Snippet" and type in your description. Follow the guidelines gives by YOAST and if you get an orange or green light you're good to go.

Use short URLs for your pages with target keywords.
Include your top keyword several times in your content.
Add them to your intro, conclusion, and one to two times in the content body and subheadings (H2, H3).

Add outbound links to authoritative resources.
Don't be afraid to link to external content sources and influencers.

Write a unique image description in ALT for at least one to two of your first images.
Google often looks through the information in ALT to understand what your content is about. So make sure to go into your Wordpress Media Library and fill in the ALT description.

Section V

CONTENT PROMOTIONAL PATHWAYS

You can have the best content plan but still fail because you're not getting enough eyeballs on it. This is why promotion is a critical champion in your content planning efforts.

Ever heard of the 80/20 rule? You should spend 20% of your time writing your content and 80% promoting it.

But before we talk about promotion, you need to prime your posts for shareability. Doing this will give you better results from your promotion strategy.

Five ways to prime your posts for shareability

Make your posts 'scanner friendly.'
I touched on this in the earlier section. You want to keep readers on your post long enough for them to make a decision whether it's a worthy piece of content that deserves a share. For that, your post needs to be 'scanner friendly' and inviting.

Use big text and a clear font. Size 12 works for paper but you would likely need a larger font size for digital. Haven't you heard that 14 is the 'new size 12'?

Add sub-heads that break the post down and give them plenty of white space as well.

Add Click-to-tweets.

Adding click-to-tweets makes your content more shareable and I've definitely noticed an increase in shares once I started to add them regularly to my posts. You can download the Better click-to-tweet plugin for free or go to the Click to Tweet site.

Add social share buttons.

Add these buttons to the top and bottom of your posts. There are several tools that allow you to add social share buttons such as Shareaholic and Social Warfare. Some tools like Social Warfare will also allow you to choose when to display the share count of a post.

Showing share counts is good for social proof. The higher the number, the more people are likely to share because of something called 'herd mentality.' If 800 other people have found this post worthy of a share, then others are more likely to share without hesitation.

Don't add all social platform share buttons to your site. Too many choices and people don't take any. It also looks terribly unattractive. Pick platforms that you use and are active on.

Tailor your images for each social platform.

Different social media platforms require different sizes. Your post becomes more shareable when you create the right social media sizes.

If you're on Pinterest, you want to make it easy for someone to find the vertical image.

There have been several times when I've gone in to pin a piece of content only to find there wasn't a vertical image (or it wasn't visible). Add a pin-it button to the image you want pinned.

Create good content.
People share content that's helpful, which in turn makes them look good. You want to create a good piece of content that everyone is clamoring to share.

Chapter 12

THE FIVE DIFFERENT PROMOTIONAL PATHWAYS

There are lots of different ways you can promote your content. I'm going to share five pathways you can attempt. It'll be almost impossible to weave every single one of these into your promotional plan because you'll be spreading yourself too thin by trying to do them all.

What you need to do is figure out which pathway and ideas give you the most traction. Monitor and analyze and focus your efforts on those pathways.

Have a steady 10-15 activities you can add into your promotional plan. Once you get comfortable with these consider adding a couple of others.

These are the five main promotional pathways, and I'll walk you through each one.

- Social Media
- Outreach
- Email
- Automated
- Paid

Social Media

Pinterest is my #1 traffic source and I've had lots of success with it. Pinterest works like a search engine though a visual medium. You need to have vertical pins and a pin description which includes keywords from your content. Pinterest is a huge topic, and while I can't walk you through the setup and pinning strategies (that would be an entire book), I'll share what you can do in terms of promotion.

You can use a scheduler like Tailwind or Boardbooster to pin your images. You could also manually pin them.

- Make vertical images for each piece of content your create.

If it's a blog post, make three to five vertical images. Like I mentioned, Pinterest is a visual medium and you need to know which image type gets you the most clicks and traffic back to your blog. By making a few images you get to test this out.

- Repin old content.

Pin your content not once, but several times to your own boards.

Likewise, keep a spreadsheet so you can track which boards you've pinned your content to and which you haven't. You could also set-up a random campaign within

Board booster to repin your old content to group boards so they get a continuous stream of traffic.

- Pin to Pinterest Group boards.

Join several group boards as a contributor. Once you do, pin your images to them. But make sure you follow the rules. Several boards have limits on the number of images you can pin per day.

- Post on Instagram.

If you're active on Instagram, make multiple images with different text overlays for your posts and content.

- Submit your post to Google+.
- Submit the post to StumbleUpon.
- Share on Twitter.

The twitter feed moves really fast and only a small percentage of your followers ever see a tweet. So you can afford to tweet out your posts several times a day. You should also tweet out your click-to-tweets.

- Share on LinkedIn.

Share your content on Linkedin if it's relevant for your niche. Share your content on LinkedIn groups as well. The right LinkedIn groups can unlock huge sources of traffic.

- Share on Facebook promotion threads.

I have a schedule of Facebook group promo threads which I try not to miss. I don't just share my new posts but old content as well because not everyone would have seen it the first time.

And 'sell' your post on Facebook threads. Don't just drop a link but share a short introduction with a call to action. Give them a peek at what's behind that piece of content to get that click-through.

- Share on sites like Medium and Quora.

Outreach

- Email anyone you mentioned in the post.

Send an email to anyone whose posts you featured or linked to within your own content. I do this without fail and most people and influencers do not hesitate to share the piece of content with their audience.

Here's a template you can use:

Hi [Influencer's first name],

Hope things are going well.

I'm [your name] from [your brand].

Just wanted to let you know that I've enjoyed reading your blog and learnt a lot about [mention specific topics/articles].

I have a new blog post on [enter title]. I mentioned your [blog post/ quote] from [blog article source].

If you have a minute, would love for you to share your thoughts on the article. I appreciate your work and wanted to drop a note to let you know that I do.

Take care.

[your sign off]

- Subscribe to Help A Reporter Out (HARO) and pitch the press.

HARO sends out an email with requests from reporters. If you find a topic that fits your niche, pitch your content.

- Tag and tweet.

Tag anyone you mentioned in the post when you tweet out your content. People are most likely to retweet and share via Twitter.

- Reach out to people sharing similar content.

This is an email I received recently. They made it really easy to share their content and reached out in a non-demanding, friendly manner. You can do the same.

Hey [name],

Hope all is well!

I was searching for some information about Guest Posting when I came across this article [LINK], a post that you previously shared on twitter.

Amazing content!

It's funny, we recently published an article entitled [your content] that I think you might find interesting.

If you find our post interesting, you can also share it using this handy click-to-tweet link

[insert click-to-tweet]

Do you have any content that you would like us to share too? Just let me know! We are also open for collaboration on other opportunities :)

[your sign off]

Email

- Email your list.

I'm not a fan of sending out blog posts notifications to your list. But if you have additional exclusive content that's tied in with the topic of your post, alert your list about your latest post. Include an easy click-to-tweet within your emails for them to share it out as well.

Automated Promotion

- Automate your tweets.

I have set up my tweets to auto-loop using IFTTT. This is completely hands-free and requires no maintenance on my part other than to update any links. Every month I go and refresh the spreadsheet with new tweets to auto loop as well. I have included a tutorial of how you can do this in the bonus pack: 1HCP.ME/BONUS

I also have the Revive old post plugin, which goes through my posts and tweets them out automatically. This ensures that even my old posts and guest posts continue to get exposure on Twitter.

You can also add recipes within IFTTT to automatically cross-share your content across different social media platforms.

Paid Promotion

Paid promotion is a topic in itself. If you have a small budget, even $2-$5 a day can help you get more eyeballs on your content. Most social media platforms like Twitter, Facebook and Pinterest provide the option to run ads (or sponsored/promoted posts).

Section VI

HOW TO MANAGE YOUR EDITORIAL WORKFLOW

It takes a huge amount of work to consistently plan, manage and effectively distribute your content.

This is why batching is critical to help you save time.

It's just like baking your favorite muffins.

If you need to bake 24 muffins, you don't

1. Prepare ingredients for 1 muffin
2. Mix the ingredients according to the recipe
3. Bake the muffin
4. Let it cool
5. Clean up your kitchen
6. Repeat 24 times

You do this instead:

1. Prepare ingredients for 24 muffins
2. Mix the ingredients according to the recipe
3. Bake the 24 muffins
4. Let them cool
5. Clean up your kitchen

Simple and effective right?

The same goes for blog posts. You can come up with a blog post idea, outline it, write it and create the visuals or you could batch similar types of tasks together. This is why the One-Hour Content Plan works because you're batching content ideation. You're producing lots of ideas and content in one go.

In this section I'll share the do's and don'ts of an editorial calendar and how it's the backbone of your content planning. I'll also share a suite of tools that help with the entire editorial process from ideation to writing to promotion.

Chapter 13

DO'S AND DON'TS OF AN EDITORIAL CALENDAR

An editorial planner, put simply, is a visual representation of your content plan. It helps you see how your content is spread out over a month or quarter, how they gel with each other and if there are any gaps that you need to fill in.

Here's why you need an editorial calendar together with your content plan.

A good, robust editorial calendar keeps you consistent. If you know that you need to publish one post per week, it helps you see at a glance how your content is progressing to meet the needs for the weeks ahead.

It helps you plan ahead and gives you flexibility. If there are niche specific holidays and promotions such as Black Friday, New Year's or Mother's Day for instance, your editorial calendar will help you see how your content is building up to help promote those events successfully. You can see where in your calendar you have pockets to fill. You can then dig into your One-Hour Content Plan and slot in relevant content ideas to fill the gap.

You can make an informed decision and say 'yes' or 'no'. If you're asked to participate in an affiliate promotion or you have guest post pitches, you can view your calendar and decide if it's feasible to say yes. Remember, well planned content, ebbs and flows and gives your audience a clear picture of where you're taking them and what point you're driving at with your content.

You don't just see the sign posts but the entire roadmap. An editorial calendar helps you take a step back and view your entire content marketing. If all of your last four pieces of content are list posts, your content calendar will help you decide if you need to inject some diversity into it and mix things up.

Here are major mistakes that still may occur after you commit to using an editorial calendar.

1. Not tracking analytics
Combining your calendar and analytics gives you powerful insight into the type of content that your audience is attracted to. It helps you see which content has the most success converting readers into subscribers. It also helps you see which content pieces have been highly shared. You can then consider replicating the success of these pieces.

2. Not having a singular swipe file

We spoke about a swipe file in Section III.

You may be collecting and saving ideas from a few different places but it's important to do a regular sieve through of these ideas and then house them in a single place. I've personally made this mistake where I've kept multiple files and notebooks for ideas. Several ideas have possibly slipped through the cracks as a result of that. I suggest having a regular look at your ideas and putting them together in a central place.

3. Not using it enough and going by memory

Using an editorial calendar takes practice. Even if you commit to using an editorial calendar, you're bound to falter at one point or another. You need to start weaving your editorial calendar into your daily work and planning so that it becomes a habit. If you're a paper and pen person, I suggest keeping your editorial calendar prominently on your desk. If you're using Google calendar or spreadsheets, commit to locking down dates in your calendar as soon as you confirm them via email.

Setting up an editorial calendar

There are two aspects to setting up an editorial calendar.

1. Choosing the type of calendar

Will you use paper, a spreadsheet or a plugin?

There are many different options.

I personally prefer to track my workflow for each piece of content and see how it comes together in a monthly overview. For instance, does the content need to be edited? Are the visuals done? Is it ready to be published? I also prefer to look back at my calendar and track my analytics for the different content pieces. I use the Create Planner which helps me do all of this in a singular place. You can find out more at CREATEPLANNER.COM

Here are some other options:

Wordpress Editorial Calendar Plugin – This free plugin works right with your WordPress site,

and you can drag and drop different posts if you want to make a change. Adding in a new

entry is as simple as clicking on a date in the calendar and clicking on 'New Post'. This will activate a quick pop-up which allows you to key in the title and details of the post.

Google Calendar/Spreadsheet – You can make changes and update them in real-time. You can also use IFTTT (If this then that) to automate updates and events in your calendar.

There are also paid options like Coschedule, which have more functionality such as scheduling social media posts once a blog post goes live.

Choose an option that you see yourself using in the long run and that you're comfortable with.

2. Content Planning - Filling the Calendar

You've already done the heavy lifting by determining the type of content ideas that will feed your calendar. You know exactly why you're creating this piece of content. They either fit in with your goals for the month or quarter, help to promote your products and services or inch your audience towards the change that your blog advocates. If you recall, we spoke about each of these aspects in Section III.

Chapter 14

TOOLS TO MANAGE AN EDITORIAL WORKFLOW

Content organization

Workflowy – An organizational tool that makes creating lists and taking notes easy

Coggle – Coggle makes mind mapping easy, and the free version is more than sufficient for simple projects.

Mindmeister – Explore more mind-mapping options with Mindmeister. This takes you a while longer to get the hang of it but gives you more features and templates compared to Coggle.

Skitch – Make easy Annotations and mark-ups with Skitch This is a free tool by the people at Evernote. I use it every single day for my blog posts and occasionally when I work with VAs or developers.

Headline Analyzers and Generators

Co-schedule Headline Analyzer – This tools analyzes headlines and titles and provides feedback on length and word choice. Run a few title options through the Headline Analyzer to see how you could make it better.

AMI Headline Analyzer – Analyzes headline based on its emotional marketing value.

Portent's Content Idea Generator – Generates headlines based on your subject. Just type in your subject and it will create a headline for you!

SEOPressor's Blog Title Generator – Provides endless catchy titles for your blog posts based on the keyword you want to write about.

Tweak Your Biz Title Generator– This is another good headline generator to use for blog posts. Just enter your topic, select whether it is a noun or a verb, and choose how you would like to capitalize words.

Keyword and content optimization tools
Yoast SEO Plugin: You need to optimize your content for search engines to rank for the right keywords and drive relevant traffic to your pages. Yoast SEO helps you optimize all relevant aspects of on-page SEO to get your site ranked and visited more often.

Ubersuggest, Keyword Tool and Keywordshitter are other tools to help you with keyword research.

StoryBase – This is a keyword tool that can help you create better headlines. When you type in your keyword, it will display a list of common phrases and questions that include your keyword.

Editing

Hemingway App - Makes your writing bold and clear. The app highlights lengthy, complex sentences and common errors.

Grammarly – There are paid and free versions that eliminate grammatical errors and enhance your writing.

Visual Marketing

Canva - Has a range of templates that make design easy.

BeFunky – Want the ease of Canva and also the ability to save templates and upload your own fonts? Befunky, an online photo editor allows you to use your own fonts and save templates.

Distraction Free Writing

Inbox Pause: Send out emails without letting new emails distract you. It sets up a pause button, click it and you're good to go.

Rescuetime – Dial into where time is lost with this app. Do this for a week or more. This app runs in the background and gives you a report on which websites you are spending your time on.

StayFocused – Block out distracting sites with this tool. Now that you know which sites are causing you time and focus, cut them out. This Chrome extension blocks everything other than what you're working on for a period of time that you specify.

CONCLUSION + NEXT STEPS

In the last few sections you discovered how to set yourself up for content success, flesh out a year's worth of blog post ideas in an hour, and package your content so that you attract an audience. You're also armed with some of the best tools to help you do so.

You have everything you need to create a solid content plan for your blog. In this concluding chapter we'll talk about what your next steps should be to maximize your content and promotional strategies.

It's useful now to take a step back and see how everything comes together in a visual overview.

The diagram below shows you how different types of content fuel the reader's journey. We spoke about this in detail in Section III. It also shows you the inextricably close relationship between email and content. It's beyond the scope of this book to cover email marketing strategies, but I want to take this opportunity get you to think about how you can take your content plan further. You will already be attracting a targeted audience to your site with the strategies you implemented with this book.

Going forward, what you essentially want to do is convert that attention. You want to get people who are already on your site and enjoying your content to become subscribers. This will give you the opportunity to continually communicate with your readers.

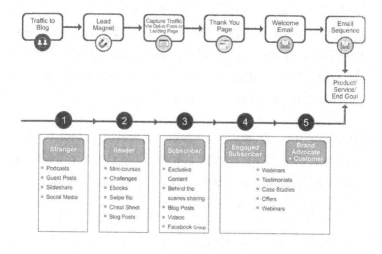

You want to gain permission to communicate with them without them having to seek you out on their own terms.

You want to capture that traffic you've attracted onto your email list. Because traffic alone is not a good purpose to have unless you're solely relying on ads or sponsored posts as a revenue model. What's the point of having 1,000 people on your site at any one time and have them leave three minutes later?

Yes, you get a nice spike in your Google Analytics, maybe some brand awareness that your blog and you exist in the online space. But what happens after that? How does traffic contribute to the goals of your blog and business?

For most of us, our blogs are used to support a service, a community, a digital product, a brick and mortar store, a membership site or an online product based business. By capturing your audience and converting them to subscribers you get permission to build a relationship with them, nurture them and prime them to do business with you. Email marketing is a must have strategy even for bloggers and solopreneurs - not just B2B or B2C companies.

The diagram above together with the One-Hour Content Plan will give you a solid foundation for marketing your blog and business. They're both designed to take the pain out of content planning and to simplify the entire process.

Many of the ideas that I spoke about in this book are not unique. But like I mentioned earlier on in the book, this is an entirely different way of thinking about content that most bloggers and small business owners are not used to.

The next time you sit down with a blog post topic, ask yourself: What goal does this piece of content fulfill? Think back to the intangible and tangible goals that we discussed in the first section. Think about how it fits into your blog and business. Every piece of content needs to have a takeaway that chips away at your reader's core problem and helps them solve it. This will allow you to work on your blog and business and not 'in' it because your content pulls its weight. It works harder for you.

I hope you give your blog a simple content strategy and a fighting chance of standing out in your niche.

Before you go, remember to download your bonuses at 1HCP.ME/BONUS

Good luck and thank you for sharing your work with the world!

THANK YOU FOR READING

I hope you enjoyed reading this book.

I really appreciate your feedback, and I love hearing what you have to say.

Could you leave me a review on Amazon letting me know what you thought of the book?

Thank you so much! If you want to get in touch, come find me here at my slice of the internet: www.meerakothand.com

Meera

RESOURCES

AMI Headline Analyzer –
http://www.aminstitute.com/headline/

BeFunky – https://www.befunky.com/

Blog Title Generator – http://seopressor.com/blog-title-generator/

Canva – http://canva.com

Copyblogger - http://www.copyblogger.com/seductive-web-copy/

www.copyblogger.com/seductive-web-copy/

www.copyblogger.com/the-two-most-important-words-in-blogging/

Co-schedule Headline Analyzer –
http://coschedule.com/headline-analyzer

Coggle – https://coggle.it/

Content Idea Generator –
https://www.portent.com/tools/title-maker

Create Planner –http://www.createplanner.com

Grammarly – https://www.grammarly.com/

Hemingway App – http://www.hemingwayapp.com/

Inbox Pause – http://inboxpause.com/

Keyword Tool – http://keywordtool.io

Keywordshitter – http://keywordshitter.com/

Mindmeister – https://www.mindmeister.com

on-page SEO – https://moz.com/ugc/category/on-page-seo

Rescuetime – https://www.rescuetime.com/ref/893136

Skitch – https://evernote.com/skitch/

Skitch – https://evernote.com/skitch/?var=c

StayFocused – https://chrome.google.com/webstore/detail/stayfocusd/laankejkbhbdhmipfmgcngdelahlfoji

StoryBase – https://www.storybase.com/

Tweak Your Biz Title Generator – http://tweakyourbiz.com/tools/title-generator/

Ubersuggest – https://ubersuggest.io/

Workflowy – https://workflowy.com

Yoast SEO – https://wordpress.org/plugins/wordpress-seo/